W9-BWF-460

DATE DUE

The Library of
HOLIDAYS™

Halloween

Amy Margaret

The Rosen Publishing Group's
PowerKids Press™
New York

Published in 2002 by The Rosen Publishing Group, Inc.
29 East 21st Street, New York, NY 10010

First Edition

Book design: Michael Caroleo and Michael de Guzman

Project Editor: Jennifer Quasha

Photo credits: p. 4 © Phyllis Picardi/International Stock; p. 7 © M. Godfrey/The Image Works; p. 8 © R. Lucas/The Image Works; p. 11 © Topham/The Image Works; p. 12 © Archive Photos; p. 15 © Lambert/Archive Photos; p. 16 © Bill Mitchell/Archive Photos; p. 19 © James L. Amos/CORBIS; p. 20 (bat) Joe McDonald/CORBIS; p. 20 (owl) DigitalStock; p. 22 © Joseph Sohm; ChromoSohm Inc./CORBIS.

Margaret, Amy.
    Halloween / Amy Margaret. —1st ed.
        p. cm. — (The library of the holidays)
    ISBN 0-8239-5782-9 (lib. binding)
1. Halloween—Juvenile literature. [1. Halloween. 2. Holidays.] I. Title. II. Series.
GT4965 .M254 2001
394.2646—dc21
                                                                00-011110

Manufactured in the United States of America

Contents

Halloween Fun

Halloween is a fun holiday. It is a time to enjoy the sweets you collect trick-or-treating. You also can dress up in a funny or scary costume. You can carve a pumpkin with a parent's help and can hang fake cobwebs from doorways. You can make a ghost out of a bedsheet. Halloween is also a time for parties. You can tell ghost stories and play games. Many of the **traditions** and **symbols** of Halloween come from other holidays celebrated thousands of years ago.

◀ *This is a house decorated for Halloween.*

Halloween's Beginnings

The earliest holiday connected with Halloween is the Celtic **festival** of **Samhain**, the Celtic New Year. The **Celts** lived in northern Europe in the first century B.C. The Celts believed in many gods, including Samhain, the Lord of the Dead. The Celts believed that Samhain ruled for six months of each year, starting on October 31, the date we now celebrate Halloween. The Celts welcomed Samhain with a three-day party. They wore costumes and searched for ghosts.

Ceremonies such as this Druid ceremony have been celebrated for more than seven hundred years. ▶

The Name Halloween

On November 1 in the year A.D. 83, the **Catholic** church gave new meaning to the Samhain holiday. They began celebrating All Saints' Day, a holiday where they honored the Catholic saints. All Saints' Day also is called All Hallows' Day or Hallowmas. Hallow means "saint" in Old English. Halloween means "Hallows' **Eve**," or the night before All Hallows' Day. October 31 was first called All Hallows' Eve, then Hallowe'en. Today Halloween is spelled without the apostrophe.

◀ *Gravestones often are decorated for All Saints' Day.*

Halloween Ghosts

Ghosts have always been an important part of Halloween. It started with the Celts, who lit fires to guide friendly ghosts home and drive away scary ghosts. Later the **Christians** celebrated their own holiday to pray for the ghosts of their dead friends or relatives. This day, November 2, was called All Souls' Day. Latin Americans call this holiday the Day of the Dead. In America, ghosts as a Halloween symbol came first from the Celts and later from the Christians. Today kids dress up as ghosts.

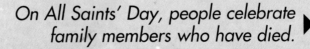

On All Saints' Day, people celebrate family members who have died. ▶

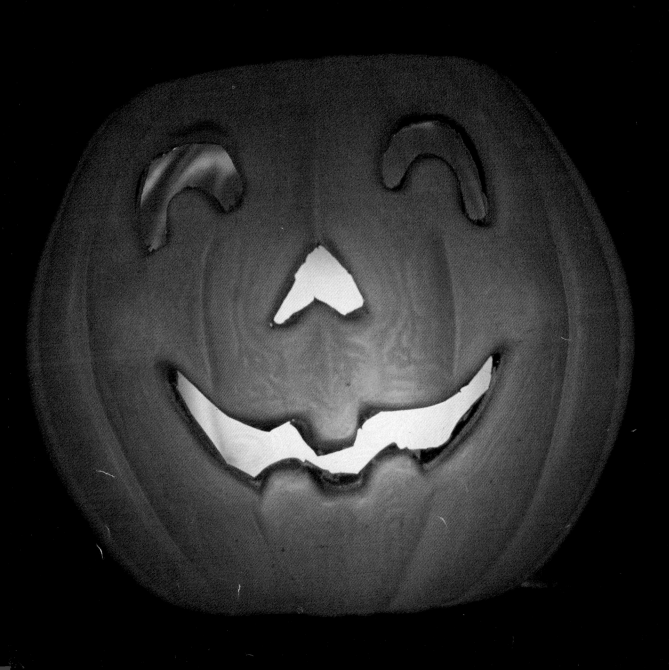

The Jack-O'-Lantern

A **jack-o'-lantern** is one of the most famous symbols of Halloween. Irish and Scottish people first used turnips as jack-o'-lanterns on Halloween. They believed that the scary faces they carved would scare away evil spirits. No one knows for sure how the jack-o'-lantern got its name. One story says that a man named Jack played tricks on the devil. When Jack died, the devil made him walk the Earth with only a piece of glowing coal to find his way. Jack carried the coal in a hollow turnip.

When the Irish and Scottish people came to America in the 1800s, they began using pumpkins for jack-o'-lanterns instead of turnips.

Trick or Treat!

Today many children in America go trick-or-treating on Halloween and shout "Trick or treat!" This phrase, first used in the United States in the 1930s, means "Give me a treat or I'll play a trick on you." The idea of going trick-or-treating probably began in England. On All Souls' Day, children went from house to house and asked for soul cakes, which were buns filled with raisins. If the children were not given food, they would pull a **prank** on that house. If they received cakes, they promised to pray for that household's dead relatives.

A group of trick-or-treaters finds a welcoming neighbor. ▶

The World of Witches

The Celts were among the first to believe in witches. A witch is someone who follows the Wiccan **faith**. In Old English, "wicca" meant "wise one." Witches used herbs and plants to heal illness. Many people thought witches had magical powers. Over time, some people thought that witchcraft was evil instead of magical. Halloween witches became symbols of the evil spirits that some people believe **wander** the Earth. People who practice the Wiccan faith, though, are different from Halloween witches.

◀ *When witches met on October 31, today's Halloween, they would perform marriages and bring new witches into their group.*

17

The Black Cat

In ancient Egypt, people believed that cats had magical powers. A **mythical** goddess named Hecate ruled over witches in ancient Greece and Rome. Hecate had a cat that helped her rule. Some people believe that witches have animals, called familiars, that assist them. The familiars have spirits living inside them. The most common familiar is the cat. A witch with her black cat is one of the most famous symbols of Halloween.

Witches' cats were black, some people thought, because the cats were evil spirits the color of night.

Halloween Creatures

The owl is another animal linked with Halloween. In the 1500s, people believed that owls were wicked. When the owl screeched, it was supposed to mean that someone had died. Another creature connected with Halloween is the bat. People associate bats with the **vampire**, a mythical monster that some believe drinks human blood. There is a bat called the vampire bat. It probably has this name because it gets its food from drinking the blood of other animals.

Owls and vampire bats may look scary, but they are not dangerous.

Play Parties

   The first American Halloween parties were called play parties. In the early 1800s, Americans celebrated fall with play parties. People played games such as bobbing for apples. Nuts sometimes were put into a small fire to tell the future. This is why some people called Halloween Nutcrack Night. Late into the night at play parties, people gathered to tell ghost stories. Today games and ghost stories are two reasons why Halloween remains one of the most popular holidays.

Glossary

Catholic (KATH-lik) Having to do with the Roman Catholic faith.

Celts (KELTS) Early European people.

Christians (KRIS-chunz) People who follow the teachings of Jesus Christ and the Bible.

eve (EEV) The evening or day before a holiday or other important day.

faith (FAYTH) A belief without proof.

festival (FES-tih-vul) A day or special time of rejoicing.

jack-o'-lantern (JAK-oh-lan-tern) A pumpkin carved to look like a face.

mythical (MITH-uh-kul) Having to do with made-up stories to explain events in nature or people's history.

prank (PRANK) A playful act meant to tease someone.

Samhain (SOW-in) Festival to celebrate the Celtic New Year.

symbols (SIM-bulz) Objects or designs that stand for something important.

traditions (truh-DIH-shunz) Ways that are passed down through the years.

vampire (VAM-pyre) A monster believed to suck the blood of animals and humans.

wander (WAHN-der) To walk from place to place without aim.

Index

A
All Saints' Day, 9
All Souls' Day, 10, 14

B
bat, 21

C
Catholic, 9
cats, 18
Celts, 6, 10, 17
Christians, 10
costume(s), 5, 6

F
familiars, 18

festival, 6

G
ghost(s), 5, 6, 10, 22

H
Hecate, 18

J
jack-o'-lantern, 13

O
owl, 21

P
play parties, 22

prank, 14
pumpkin, 5

S
Samhain, 6, 9
symbol(s), 5, 10, 13, 17, 18

T
trick-or-treating, 5, 14

V
vampire, 21

W
witches, 17, 18

Web Sites

To learn more about Halloween, check out these Web sites:
www.holidays.net/halloween/
www.theholidayspot.com/halloween/